Portraits of a Lady

An illustrated life of Frances, Countess of Warwick.

For Felice Spurrier

PORTRAITS OF A LADY

by

David Buttery

BREWIN BOOKS

First published July 1988 by
Brewin Books, Studley, Warwickshire B80 7LG
Reprinted December 1988
Reprinted September 1996

© David Buttery 1988

All rights reserved.

ISBN 0 947731 43 1

Typeset in Baskerville 11pt and
made and printed in Great Britain
by Supaprint (Redditch)Ltd., Redditch. Worcs.

"For women are as roses, whose fair flower,
   Being once displayed, doth fall that very hour."

                          William Shakespeare

"Take ye your pleasure at the best,
  Be merry, ere your beauty flit;
  For length of days will tarnish it,
  Like roses that were loveliest."

                          Pierre De Ronsard

"— There's a daisy:- "

                          William Shakespeare

"Strew on her roses, roses,
  And never a spray of yew!
  In quiet she reposes;
  Ah, would that I did too!"

                          Matthew Arnold

ACKNOWLEDGEMENTS

Copyright reserved. Reproduced by gracious permission of Her Majesty The Queen, 5, 11, 24. Country Life 7. Musee Rodin 27. National Portrait Gallery 8. Royal Commission on the Historic Monuments of England 19. Warwickshire and Worcestershire Life 6. Worcester Art Museum, Worcester, Massachusetts, U.S.A. 20. All other photographs are from the author's collection.

ILLUSTRATIONS

Frontispiece. Miss Frances Evelyn (Daisy Maynard), pencil portrait with daisies by George Francis (Frank) Miles, 1877.

1. Miss Frances Evelyn Maynard and her sister Blanche, painting by Aster Corbould, 1871. Private Collection   11

2. Miss Frances Evelyn Maynard, tinted photograph by H.S. Mendelssohn, c. 1879. Private Collection.   12

3. The wedding of Francis Greville Lord Brooke and Miss Frances Evelyn Maynard. Illustrated London News, May 7, 1881.   13

4. Lady Brooke (Daisy), photograph by Walery, c.1881.   14

5. Lady Brooke, bust in marble by Giovanni Amendola, 1883. Warwick Castle Collection.   15

6. Easton Lodge: the west wing, 1907.   16

7. Lady Brooke, photograph by Walery, c. 1885   19

8. Easton Lodge: the Stone Hall, 1898.   20

9. Easton Lodge: the Stone Hall topiary sundial, c. 1905.   21

10. Lady Brooke, photograph by Walery, 1890.   22

11. Warwick Castle: the east front, c. 1900.   23

12. Warwick Castle: the south front, c. 1900.   24

13. Warwick Castle: the Great Hall, c. 1880.   27

14. Warwick Castle: the Great Hall, c. 1900.   28

15. Warwick Castle: Lady Warwick's (Daisy's) Boudoir, 1897.   29

16. The Costume Ball (Bal Poudre) at Warwick Castle, 1895.   30

17. Lady Warwick, painting by Carolus-Duran, 1897. Private Collection.   31

18. Warwick Castle: the Red Drawing Room, c.1900.   32

19. Lady Warwick and her Son Maynard, painting by John Singer Sargent, 1905. Worcester Art Museum, Massachusetts, U.S.A.   35

20. Warwick Castle: the Cedar Drawing Room, watercolour by W.W. Quatremaine, c. 1909.   36

21. Lady Warwick, photograph by Fellows Willson, 1905.   37

22. Easton Lodge: Lady Warwick's Bedroom, c. 1905.   38

23. Easton Lodge: Lady Warwick's Sitting-Room, c.1890.   39

24. Lady Warwick, pastel by Ellis Roberts, c. 1899. Private Collection.   40

25. Lady Warwick, photograph, c. 1905.   43

26. Lady Warwick, bust in marble by Auguste Rodin, 1908. Musee Rodin, Paris.   44

27. Easton Lodge: the Pond Garden, c.1905.   45

28. Lady Warwick with retired circus ponies at Easton Lodge.   46

Miss Frances Evelyn (Daisy Maynard), pencil portrait with daisies by George Francis (Frank) Miles, 1877.

PORTRAITS OF A LADY

In our time it has come to seem strange and perhaps unfashionable to see a woman not as a person but simply as an image. In fact, this has always been the way women have been seen, both in art and photography. The late nineteenth century witnessed great developments in photographic techniques with the windows of the photographers studios filled with portraits of the celebrities and beautiful women of the day. Thus photography took its place alongside painting and sculpture as a form of portraiture. These developments in photography saw the emergence of what became known as the 'professional beauty' — a woman who was viewed simply as an image, an object, something to be admired, desired, gazed upon. Of these ladies which formed so brilliant a part of the English scene in the closing years of 'la belle epoque' one of the finest was certainly Frances Evelyn, fifth Countess of Warwick.

In writing of Lady Warwick one is drawn always to the idea of her as a simply beautiful woman, a presence, perhaps even a body. Though her life, with its dramatic and contradictory aspects, is full of interest, it is to the physical reality of her person that one is inevitably drawn back. In essence her existence was as nothing compared to the quality of her portrayal and it is for this quality that she deserves to be remembered. Today, we live in an age when, to produce an effect, a lady will undress, yet Frances Warwick never needed to do this as may be seen from the photographs of her. These photographs, the paintings and sculptures for which she sat, and the lost glories of the great houses and gardens in which she lived provide a poignant glimpse of a great beauty now faded and gone.

The fifth Countess of Warwick was born Frances Evelyn Maynard on the 10 December, 1861. The Maynard family had risen to prominence in Tudor times and had also enjoyed the favour of the Stuarts. In 1766, George III, had granted the family the title of Viscount and Frances Evelyn's own father was the only son of the third Maynard to hold the title. Her mother, Blanche Fitzroy, was a cousin of the Duke of Grafton — a relationship which was to enable Frances Evelyn to claim Nell Gwyn amongst her ancestors.

Though born in London, Frances or Daisy as she was

known from her earliest years, perhaps because of her richness of fair hair, spent her childhood at the Maynard family seat of Easton Lodge in Essex, now demolished. Daisy's father died when she was just four years old and she was left with only one younger sister, Blanche. The following year, 1866, her mother remarried, her second husband being the fourth Earl of Rosslyn, this marriage was to provide Daisy with four step-sisters and one step-brother. Lord Rosslyn's home was at Dysart House in Scotland and here Daisy spent many happy summers and could visit the romantic castle of Ravenscraig — romantic castles, both real and in the air, were to form a theme of her life. When at Easton Lodge she was educated by governesses of whom the best was Miss Blake who taught her to speak French and German fluently. Her chief love was however, for the countryside and for horses and it is no accident that her first portrait, that by Aster Corbould, shows Daisy mounted upon her pony with her sister Blanche standing beside. (pl. 1).

At Easton Lodge Daisy was to grow up a most beautiful and striking young woman. This may be clearly seen from a drawing by the artist Frank Miles (frontispiece) which shows her aged sixteen, and a later tinted photograph by the noted Victorian portrait photographer H.S. Mendelssohn (pl. 2). This photograph, perhaps the finest ever taken of Daisy, reveals her graceful figure and carriage and the stunning even chilling sense she could produce. The dress has a pattern of daisies embroidered at the neck in allusion to her love-name. At nineteen, Daisy was in great demand as an Essex newspaper reported: "She is as beautiful as she is good . . . the photographers are pursuing her." Later, her half-brother Harry Rosslyn was to write that she: ". . . had the world at her feet . . . she was recognized as one of the most beautiful girls this country has ever produced."

Curiously, Daisy felt herself to be plain and, as she was to write in her memoirs: "In my teens, it came as a deep and almost incredible surprise and delight to me to find in men's eyes an unfailing tribute to a beauty I myself had not been able to discern." Even writing after some fifty years one may still feel the sense of satisfaction and power which the dawning awareness of her beauty brought her. The importance to a woman of physical beauty then as now cannot be overestimated. As Daisy

10

1. Miss Frances Evelyn Maynard and her sister Blanche, painting by Aster Corbould, 1871. Private Collection.

2. Miss Frances Evelyn Maynard, tinted photograph by H.S. Mendelssohn, c. 1879. Private Collection.

3. The wedding of Francis Greville Lord Brooke and Miss Frances Evelyn Maynard. Illustrated London News, May 7, 1881.

4. Lady Brooke (Daisy), photograph by Walery, c.1881.

5. Lady Brooke, bust in marble by Giovanni Amendola, 1883. Warwick Castle Collection.

6. Easton Lodge: the west wing, 1907.

wrote: "I was a beauty and only those who were alive then know the magic that word held for the period."

Daisy's grandfather, Henry Viscount Maynard, survived for a short time his own son, Daisy's father. Much to the chagrin of his other relatives Henry Maynard, in his will, made Daisy the principal beneficiary. Thus she was to find herself not only very beautiful but also very rich. As Montagu Corry, private secretary to the Prime Minister, Benjamin Disraeli, observed: "The heiress — Miss Daisy — is growing into a fine young woman. She is now fifteen, so that for three years she will not be the talk of London . . . her fortune will be much over £30,000 a year. Whatever it be, I see she will bestow it upon whomsoever she chooses — and turn out a maitresse femme." Clearly, even at this early age, Daisy was making her presence and strength of character felt.

When Daisy did 'come out' into society the effect was, as Montagu Corry had predicted, immediate. Later she was to write of this time: "I was feted, feasted, courted and adored . . ." This irresistable combination of beauty and money attracted the attention of Queen Victoria and, for a time, Daisy was considered as a possible bride for the Queen's youngest son, Prince Leopold. Disraeli, now Lord Beaconsfield, was particularly keen on this marriage and strove to advance it but, in the event, Leopold's affections lay elsewhere. Meanwhile, Daisy had attracted the interest of Francis Lord Brooke, the eldest son and heir to the fourth Earl of Warwick and his historic home of Warwick Castle. Daisy's mother and stepfather did not entirely welcome Lord Brooke's attachment since they hoped for the Royal Marriage. Nevertheless, Brooke who was quite overwhelmed by Daisy's blonde tresses and dark blue eyes, succeeded, with Prince Leopold's help, in proposing under a large umbrella on a wet afternoon near the Prince's home of Claremont in Surrey.

Daisy's wedding to Lord Brooke took place in Westminster Abbey on the 30 April, 1881, and was a great occasion with the Prince and Princess of Wales as the principal guests. Mary Elizabeth Lucy of Charlecote Park was also a guest and noted in her Journal: ". . . the bride came leaning on Lord Rosslyn's arm, looking 'simple perfection' in an exquisite dress of white satin duchess lace and fringes of orange flowers. She carried a great bouquet of Marechal Niel roses." (pl. 4) Lord and Lady

Brooke spent their honeymoon at Ditton Park on the Thames loaned to them by the Duke of Buccleuch, and it was from there that they were summoned to dinner with Queen Victoria at Windsor Castle. Her Majesty noted in her Journal: "Lady Brooke (formerly Miss Maynard, the pretty young bride, married a fortnight ago) came over from Ditton . . . Little Ldy. Brooke, in her wedding gown trimmed with most beautiful lace and orange flowers, looked so simple and unaffected." The Queen was so taken with Daisy that she took a spray of orange blossom from her dress to keep as a souvenir and requested that she should be photographed, one of these photographs is still in the Royal Archives (pl. 4). Two years after her marriage, Daisy, sat to a sculptor for the first time the artist being the Italian Giovanni Amendola (pl. 5). This bust, which was exhibited at the Royal Academy in 1883, reveals her beautiful neck and shoulders.

In the years following her marriage, Daisy, made her home at Easton Lodge (pl. 6). Though originally dating from the end of the sixteenth century, the Lodge had been rebuilt in Elizabethan style following a fire in 1847, Daisy was to make it a place of splendid entertainment. One of her guests was the novelist Elinor Glyn and she was later to write: "No one who stayed at Easton ever forgot their hostess, and most of the men fell hopelessly in love with her . . . I have seen most of the beautiful and famous women of the world . . . I have never seen one who was so completely fascinating as Daisy Brooke." Though much of Daisy's time was spent on the round of country house parties she rapidly found the attractions of such occasions waning. She joined that somewhat raffish element which formed around the Prince of Wales and which was known as "the Marlborough House Set." Daisy recalled the gardens at Marlborough House as providing: "the finest surroundings for flirtation to be found in the Metropolis." Of these times she was later to write: "We would dine late and long, trifle with the Opera for an hour or so, or watch the ballet at the Empire, then 'go on' to as many houses as we could crowd in . . . As for money, our only understanding of it lay in the spending, not in the making of it."

If, during the eighteen-eighties, it became clear that Daisy was becoming bored with conventional society, it also became obvious that no mere husband could satisfy

7. Lady Brooke, photograph by Walery, c. 1885.

8. Easton Lodge: the Stone Hall, 1898.

9. Easton Lodge: the Stone Hall topiary sundial, c.1905.

10. Lady Brooke, photograph by Walery, 1890.

11. Warwick Castle: the east front, c. 1900.

12. Warwick Castle: the south front, c. 1900.

her beautiful person and passionate nature. Thus it was that she pursued an affair with the dashing naval officer, Lord Charles Beresford, much to the chagrin of his wife. Beresford may perhaps be forgiven when one realizes what an impressive figure Daisy made at this time (pl. 7). In 1884 he deserted her to serve on the mission that vainly tried to rescue General Gordon from Khartoum. If Beresford was, perhaps, the most adventurous of Daisy's lovers he was far from being the only one, for she numbered amongst them no lesser person than the Prince of Wales himself, the future King Edward the Seventh.

Precisely when the Prince and Daisy became lovers is not certain. Prince Edward was a regular visitor to Easton Lodge during the eighteen-eighties where a charming Tudor house in the park, known as the Stone Hall (pl. 8), provided an ideal venue for assignations. With its small but exquisite garden, one feature of which was a topiary sundial (pl. 9), the Stone Hall must have provided a delightful setting for romance. The sundial was planted, appropriately if ambiguously, to read: "Les heures heureuses ne se comptent pas" — when one is happy one does not count the hours.

As is well-known, Daisy was not the Prince of Wales' only mistress since he had already enjoyed the favours of the famous Victorian beauty, Mrs. Langtry. Daisy had actually met Lily Langtry in 1877 and she had become something of an obsession for her stepfather, Lord Rosslyn and was often at his London house and at Easton. Many year later Daisy was to write that Lily Langtry was the loveliest woman she had ever seen. That she could herself easily stand comparison with the "Jersey Lily" is shown by a photograph taken by Walery, the Royal Photographer, and which she probably gave to Prince Edward since it remains in the Royal Archives (pl. 10). In this photograph, which she actually signed "Frances Evelyn Brooke" she stands and displays her magnificent figure. This portrait of Daisy reveals that glory of the Victorian beauty, the literally breath taking effect of her wasp-waist.

As a rich, beautiful, aristocratic woman, mistress of the Prince of Wales, Daisy had the social world at her feet. This triumph was well described in a society periodical of May 1891: "At the Opera the Prince of Wales with his two younger daughters. Lady Brooke was in the pit tier, and the writer craned her neck to catch a glimpse of the goddess whose fame has penetrated even to the dim recess of the placid countryside. Her profile was turned away from an inquisitive world, but I made out a rounded figure, diaphanously draped, and a brilliant beautiful countenance." Daisy's position in society was further increased when, in 1893, her father-in-law the fourth Earl of Warwick died and she became the fifth Countess of Warwick, chatelaine of what was then one of the great historic family seats of England, Warwick Castle (pls. 11 and 12).

Though of Norman origin, Warwick Castle had been restored in the Jacobean period and, in 1871, partially destroyed by fire. As Countess, Daisy transformed Warwick with the austere simplicity of the Great Hall (pl. 13), created following the fire, becoming a sitting-room (pl. 14). In the private apartments, not shown to the paying visitor, she had her own boudoir (pl. 15). Daisy also made the castle a scene of great occasions and, in 1895, she held a spectacular costume ball with the guests coming dressed as characters from the ages of Louis the Fifteenth and Sixteenth of France, she herself portrayed Marie Antoinette (pl. 16). Famous artists were to perform for her at the castle including the great French actress, Sarah Bernhardt, who played Hamlet in the Great Hall. Noted singers such as Clara Butt and Harry Plunket-Greene gave recitals arranged by Daisy's old music teacher, the organist and conductor Wilhelm Ganz.

Perhaps surprisingly, no portrait had been painted of Daisy prior to her succeeding as Countess of Warwick. She was to have sat, in 1895, to Frederick Lord Leighton but though he wrote of her that: "I, as an artist, should not be likely to have 'forgotten' you . . ." his death prevented the painting being executed. In 1897, whilst visiting Paris, she did sit to the French painter Carolus-Duran (pl.17). This chance almost certainly saved her life since it was an unexpected demand by the artist, for an extra sitting, which prevented her presence at a charity bazaar that experienced a severe fire in which many died. The portrait, perhaps at the wish of the Earl of Warwick, recalls those of the seventeenth century Flemish master Van Dyck. Daisy hung this painting of herself at Warwick Castle in the centre of the Red Drawing Room (pl. 18).

13. Warwick Castle: the Great Hall, c. 1880.

14. Warwick Castle: the Great Hall, c. 1900.

15. Warwick Castle: Lady Warwick's (Daisy's) Boudoir, 1897.

16. The Costume Ball (Bal Poudre) at Warwick Castle, 1895.

17. Lady Warwick, painting by Carolus-Duran, 1897. Private Collection.

18. Warwick Castle: the Red Drawing Room, c. 1900.

Carolus-Duran's finest pupil was the American portrait painter, John Singer Sargent, and in 1905 Daisy sat to him with her youngest son Maynard (pl. 19). The painting gave the artist considerable trouble, in particular capturing Daisy's beauty proved elusive. In despair, Sargent was heard to exclaim: "I've simply got to finish that damn thing. The boy keeps getting older and the woman keeps getting younger." The portrait itself reveals the influence of the eighteenth century English artist, Gainsborough, and emphasises Daisy's statuesque quality. At Warwick she hung the picture in the castle's Cedar Drawing Room where it was depicted by a local artist, William Quatremaine (pl. 20).

The portraits by Carolus-Duran and Sargent are the only paintings now known of Daisy and, though Sargent in particular created an impressive image, neither captured her dramatic quality as well as a photograph of about the same time (pl. 21). This portrait was sold as a postcard at Warwick Castle and helped to create the image of her. It is one of the most telling as well as one of the most famous pictures of Daisy revealing her beautiful complexion and finely cut features.

The great Warwick Castle costume ball of 1895 was to be a critical event in Daisy's life. Its extravagance was criticised in the socialist journal The Clarion, edited by Robert Blatchford, and Daisy, who had already an interest in socialist politics, at once set out for London to confront him. Blatchford was later to write of this meeting: "Seated in my dingy den, in my undignified garment, I was confronted with a beautiful lady, beautifully dressed, whose obvious intention was to 'Trafalgar Square' me." In the event, Blatchford, countered Daisy's wrath with his own socialist rhetoric and this was to have a powerful, if delayed, effect since Daisy eventually embraced the socialist cause herself.

Inevitably, Daisy's socialism was to be very much one of her own, perhaps typified by a remark she passed to the architect Philip Tilden when planning the restoration of Easton Lodge: "A shack will do for me, dear thing." Tilden soon discovered the shack must include within: "a Ritz-like bathroom, a most sunny, large and beautiful bedroom with a sitting room alongside." Daisy's bedroom at Easton was indeed a charming interior (pl. 22), whilst another of her rooms reveals her liking for the presence of photographs (pl. 23).

Despite its inevitable contradictions and quixotic aspects, Daisy's efforts to assist the poor and improve the opportunities for young women were not without their achievements. At Easton she established a school which gave many children the chance of higher education they would otherwise never have had. At Warwick she founded a home for disabled children and, in the Warwickshire village of Studley, an agricultural college for women. This last foundation, which survived longest, did valuable work. In her sense of conviction and willingness to act, as well as in her insistence on the need for improved education, particularly for young women, Daisy was undoubtedly correct.

In a sense Daisy's value to the socialist movement lay in her appearance and the attention she attracted. The British socialist, Henry Hyndman, recalled her as: "Tall graceful and well proportioned, with a vast mass of fair hair, clear blue eyes, and a perfect complexion, Lady Warwick might well be considered, as indeed she was, the most beautiful woman of her time." When she appeared at the socialist congress in Amsterdam during 1903 the effect was, according to Hyndman, "startling." The society pastellist, Ellis Roberts, produced a pair of drawings of Daisy and these provide a beautiful glimpse of her at about this time. One shows her formally with her hair worn 'up', whilst the other (pl. 24) has her tresses partially let down. This latter depiction is unusual for its informality and makes one regret the absence of other portraits of a similar character.

With her romances, her socialist politics, and her extravagance which led her to bankruptcy, one may wonder that the Earl of Warwick never lost patience with his Countess. In fact, he never did, and the reason for this must have lain, at least in part, with her personal charm and this is something hard to appreciate from photographs. As Philip Tilden wrote: "All people forgave her everything, for they loved her so much. Her human instincts and interests were many and marvellous, her sense of humour and infectious laugh tied one to her for life." Perhaps this quality is best caught in an informal photograph which captures that fleeting sensation of herself which made Daisy, for all her faults, so irresistible (pl. 25).

19. Lady Warwick and her Son Maynard, painting by John Singer Sargent, 1905. Worcester Art Museum, Massachusetts, U.S.A.

20. Warwick Castle: the Cedar Drawing Room, watercolour by W.W. Quatremaine, c. 1909.

21. Lady Warwick, photograph by Fellows Willson, 1905.

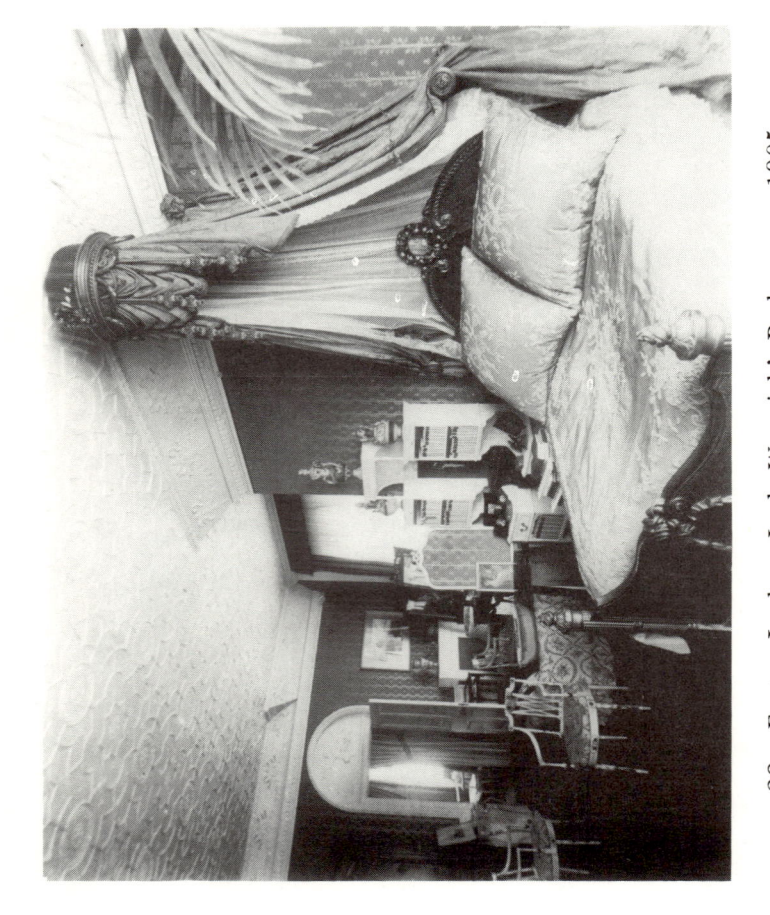

22. Easton Lodge: Lady Warwick's Bedroom, c. 1905.

23. Easton Lodge: Lady Warwick's Sitting-Room, c. 1890.

24. Lady Warwick, pastel by Ellis Roberts, c. 1899. Private Collection.

The photograph (pl. 25) was taken when Daisy was seated in an early motor car in the courtyard of Warwick Castle. She was then already over forty years old and it reveals how well she retained that loveliness so remarked upon in her youth. Hyndman, who introduced her to the French socialist Jaures, and the future Prime Minister of France, Clemenceau, recalled how: "They were both quite swept off their legs by her beauty (tho' 42 as she constantly tells people, she looks 26)." Despite this, inevitably, the passing years took their toll and in 1908, at the age of forty-seven, Daisy sat to an artist for the last time. This was to be for the French sculptor, Auguste Rodin. Two busts in marble were carved and these may have been at the request of Edward the Seventh. Daisy had actually written to Rodin in 1904 but the King is said to have visited the artist in 1908 with a beautiful English lady and, requesting a sculpture of her, paid the artist a large sum.

Rodin's portrait of Daisy (pl. 26) is perhaps the most enigmatic ever taken of her. The artist did not attempt a simple likeness but chose rather to give her features a veiled, distant, dream-like quality. In his portraiture, Rodin, believed: "The resemblance which the artist ought to obtain is that of the soul." In this way his portrait of Daisy has almost the effect of a death-mask with the features seeming raised and the eyes looking through and beyond. In this sense it suggests something of a valedictory quality as if Daisy's beauty was, even as he watched, passing away, as indeed it was.

When Daisy sat to Rodin the age of the professional beauties and the artists and photographers who had portrayed them was only a memory. These years had witnessed the zenith of both her beauty and her power as one of the great society hostesses. The latter part of Daisy's life was not to be without its difficulties and sadnesses. Her entertaining, particularly of Edward the Seventh, and her socialist schemes had cost her much capital and led to financial disaster. Estates and works of art had to be sold and Warwick Castle itself was rented to an American family, towards the end of her life money was to be very short. In 1918, Daisy's own family home of Easton Lodge was severely damaged by fire and in 1924, her husband, the fifth Earl of Warwick died. His death was followed only four years later by that of her eldest son, Leopold Guy the sixth Earl.

Despite her years as chatelaine of the castle, Daisy had never been truly happy at Warwick and, after 1914, she must have been relieved to withdraw to Easton Lodge. Daisy once described Warwick Castle as a "museum" and, on another occasion, as "a national glory" which she and her husband saw as a responsibility they must accept and discharge. Nevertheless, as her half-brother Harry Rosslyn was to observe: "her heart was always at Easton." In 1902 she had Harold Peto lay out the most beautiful gardens at the Lodge (pl. 27) and it was to be in these splendid surroundings, now all but vanished, that Daisy was to spend her final years.

At Easton socialist gatherings were held and plans for a Labour Party college discussed, amongst the visitors were Sidney Webb, his wife Beatrice, and Ramsay MacDonald. Amateur theatricals were organized with Ellen Terry and Bernard Shaw assisting. Another visitor was Lily Langtry bitterly resenting the loss of her once famous beauty. H.G. Wells resided on the estate for a time and brought such guests as Charlie Chaplin and novelists Arnold Bennett and John Galsworthy. Yet for all this activity the beauties of Easton Lodge, like those of Lily Langtry and Daisy, were to fade. Daisy herself lamented that whilst there had once been sixteen gardeners at Easton this had later to be reduced to eight. The theatrical producer, Basil Dean, who was to marry Daisy's youngest daughter Mercy, described life at Easton Lodge as: "uncontrolled amplitude faced by inexorable diminution." This diminution was to come after Daisy's death with the park becoming a Second World War airfield and the house demolished in 1949.

As with Easton Lodge itself, Daisy retained her charm even in old age though this, as a lady observed, seemed as from another world: "... her face had still the fixed pink-and-white attractions which one associates with the Lily Langtry era, and an 'electric light' smile which was turned on in a brilliant flash and gone again." In 1929, Daisy had published her memoirs in which she expressed her wish to die at Easton and nine years later, in 1938, this wish was to be granted. All her life she had been devoted

25. Lady Warwick, photograph, c. 1905.

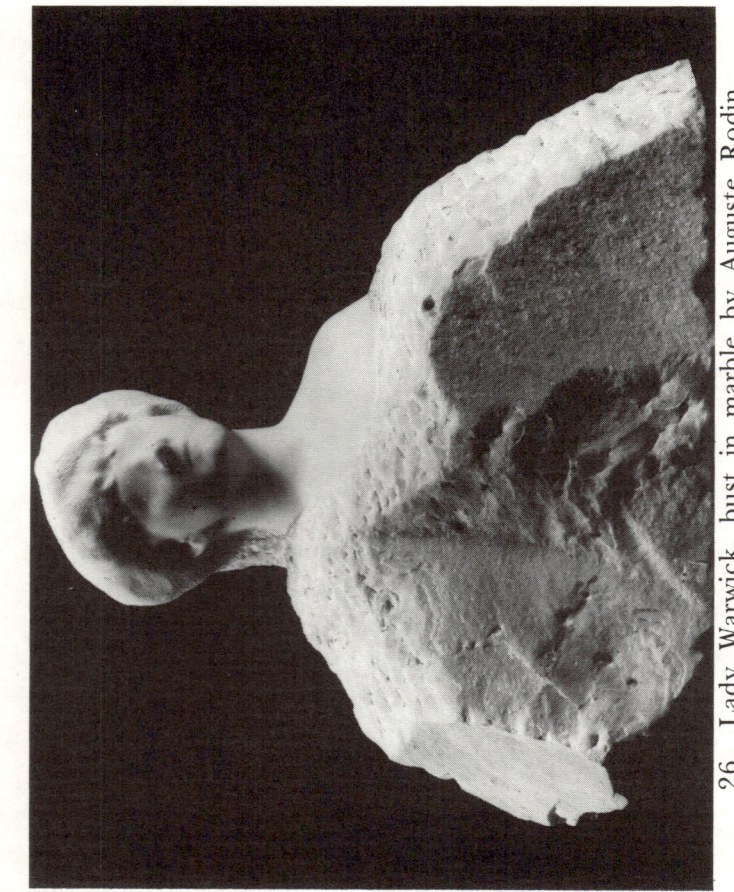

26. Lady Warwick, bust in marble by Auguste Rodin, 1908. Musee Rodin, Paris.

27. Easton Lodge: the Pond Garden, c. 1905.

28. Lady Warwick with retired circus ponies at Easton Lodge.

to horses and it is appropriate that our last glimpse of Daisy, shortly before her death, should be with the retired circus ponies to whom she gave a last home at the Lodge (pl. 28). Thus it was that Daisy's brilliant, passionate, and turbulent life was to end with her surrounded by the animals which had, perhaps, meant most to her.

FRANCES EVELYN WARWICK'S OWN WRITINGS

Lady Warwick wrote or contributed to several books and articles of which the most interesting are: An Old English Garden, published in 1898, Warwick Castle and its Earls published in 1903, Life's Ebb and Flow published in 1929, and Afterthoughts published in 1931. The first of these is an account of her lost garden at the Stone Hall of Easton Lodge and includes the quotations which appeared on the labels of the Shakespeare Border and Roserie — some of these lines appear at the beginning of this book. Warwick Castle and its Earls was written with the help of Dr. Harvey Bloom, it remains a valuable source on the lives of the Earls of Warwick. Her two volumes of memoirs, entitled Life's Ebb and Flow and Afterthoughts, provide a glimpse of life in Victorian and Edwardian England and Lady Warwick's view of it.